About the koan, *you should single out the point where you have*
been in doubt all your life and put it upon your forehead.
Is it a holy place or a commonplace one? Is it an entity or a non-entity?
Press your question to its very end. Do not be afraid of plunging yourself
into vacuity; find out what it is that cherishes the sense of fear.
Is it a void or is it not?

Tai-Hui

These training schools often employ a considerable amount of manual
labour in addition to meditative techniques, in an attempt to avoid
being bound by the mind. As the Buddha-mind is to be found in
everything there is an emphasis on a connection with action, rather
than conceptual thinking, and with the direct vision of nature rather
than an interpretation. This has exerted a profound influence on the
arts of Japan. While Zen religious painting might avoid iconography, it
portrays natural forms such as birds, grasses, rocks and mountains in a
style that combines maximum technique with minimum deliberation.

There is here, not there.
Infinity is before our eyes.

Seng T'san

This same approach affected not only painting but also poetry,
calligraphy, gardening and architecture. It is at the heart of ceremonial
tea drinking and has also influenced the arts of fencing, archery and
ju-jitsu. It is recognized as the essence behind everything.

O my good friends gathered here,
If you desire to listen to the thunderous voice of the Way,
Exhaust your words, empty your thoughts,
For then you may come to recognize this One Essence.

Dai-o Kokushi

January

January 1

Pursue not the outer entanglements,
Dwell not in the inner Void;
Be serene in the oneness of things,
And dualism vanishes by itself.

January 2

*The Great Way is calm
and large-hearted,
For it nothing is easy, nothing hard;
Small views are irresolute, the more in
haste, the tardier they go.*

January 3

*It is one's own mind that
creates illusions.
Is this not the greatest
self-contradiction?*

January 4

*A special transmission
outside the Scriptures;
No dependence on words and letters;
Direct pointing to the mind of man;
Seeing into one's own nature.*

January 5

In the higher realm of true suchness,
there is neither 'self' nor 'other':
when direct identification is sought,
we can only say 'not two'.

January 6

You should know that so far
as Buddha-nature is concerned,
there is no difference
between an enlightened man and
an ignorant one. What makes
the difference is that one realizes
it and one doesn't.

January 7

Our Essence of Mind is intrinsically pure and if we knew our mind and realized what our nature is, all of us would attain Buddhahood.

January 8

The master said to me:
'All the Buddhas and all the sentient beings
are nothing but the One Mind beside which
nothing exists. This mind, which is without
beginning, is unborn and indestructible. It is
not green nor yellow, is unborn and has
neither form nor appearance. It does not
belong to the categories of things which exist
or do not exist, nor can it be thought of as
new or old. It is neither long nor short, big
nor small, for it transcends all limits,
measures, names, traces and comparisons.
It is that which you see before you – begin to
reason about it and you at once fall into
error. It is like the boundless void which
cannot be fathomed or measured.'

January 9

The One Mind alone is the Buddha and there is no distinction between the Buddha and all sentient things, but the sentient beings are attached to forms and so seek externally for Buddhahood. By their very seeking, they lose it for that is seeking the Buddha to seek for the Buddha and using mind to grasp mind.

January 10

My way is through mind-awakening.
How can it be conveyed in words?
Speech only produces some effect
when it falls on the uninstructed
ears of children.

January 11

The pure mind, the source of everything, shines forever and on all with the brilliance of its own perfection. But the people of the world do not awaken to it, regarding only that which one sees, hears, feels and knows as mind. Blinded by their own sight, hearing, feeling, knowing, they do not perceive the spiritual brilliance of the source-substance.

Do you see that Zen student? He has forgotten what he has learned; yet he practises easily and freely what he has learned and also what he should learn.

January 13

A single bundle of thread is made up of innumerable strands; but, if you join them together in a rope and put it on a plank, you can easily cut all these threads with one stroke of a sharp knife. As many as those threads may be, they cannot resist the one blade. With those who are converted to the way of the *Bodhisattvas*, it is just the same. If they meet with a true good friend who by skilful means brings them to immediate perception of the Absolute, with diamond wisdom they cut through the passions that belong to all stages of *Bodhisattva*hood.

January 14

*A Zen student walks in
Zen and sits in Zen.
Whether in speech and
action, or silence or inaction,
his body dwells in peace.
He smiles at the sword
that takes his life.
He keeps his poise even in
the moment of death.*

January 15

If you clearly realize for yourself that
your mind does not abide anywhere
whatsoever, that is called clearly
perceiving your real mind. It is also
called clearly perceiving reality. Only
the mind which abides nowhere is the
mind of a Buddha. It can be described
as a mind set free.

January 16

A long time ago, when the World Honoured One was dwelling on Vulture Peak, he picked up a flower and showed it to the congregation. They all remained unmoved, but the venerable Mahakasyapa smiled. The Honoured One said: 'I have in my hand the doctrine of the right *Dharma* which is birthless and deathless, the true form of no-form and a great mystery. It is the message of non-dependence upon [words] and letters and is transmitted outside the scriptures. I now hand it to Mahakasyapa.'

There's a reality even prior to Heaven
and Earth; Indeed it has no form, much
less a name; Eyes fail to see it;
It has no voice for ears to detect.
To call it mind or Buddha violates its nature.
Absolutely quiet, and yet illuminating
It allows itself to be perceived only by
the clear-eyed.
It is Dharma beyond form and sound;
It is Tao without words.
Wishing to entice the blind
The Buddha has playfully let words
escape his golden mouth;
Heaven and Earth are ever since filled
with entangling briars.

January 18

Good friends, how then are meditation and wisdom alike? They are like the lamp and the light it gives forth. If there is a lamp, there is light; if there is no lamp, there is no light. The lamp is the substance of light; the light is the function of the lamp. Thus, although they have two names, in substance they are not two. Meditation and wisdom are also like this.

Two come about because of one,
but don't cling to the one either!
So long as the mind does not stir,
the ten thousand things stay blameless;
no blame, no phenomena,
no stirring, no mind.

Before I had studied Zen for thirty years, I saw mountains as mountains, and waters as waters. When I arrived at a more intimate knowledge, I came to the point where I saw that mountains are not mountains and waters are not waters. But now I have got its very substance, I am at rest. For it is just that I see mountains once again as mountains and waters once again as waters.

January 21

The master said:
'There is no special teaching:
the most ordinary things in our daily
life hide some deep meaning that is yet
most plain and explicit; only our eyes
need to see where there is a meaning.

The perfect way is without difficulty,
save that it avoids
picking and choosing.
Only when you stop liking and disliking
will all be clearly understood.

January 23

Without looking forward to tomorrow every moment, you must think only of this day and this hour. Because tomorrow is difficult and unfixed and difficult to know, you must think of living the Buddhist way whilst you live today.

January 24

Buddha told a parable in a *sutra*:
A man travelling across a field encountered a
tiger. He fled, the tiger after him. Coming to a
precipice, he caught hold of a wild vine and
swung himself down over the edge. The tiger
sniffed at him from above. Trembling, the
man looked down to where, far below,
another tiger was waiting to eat him.
Two mice, one white and one black,
little by little started to gnaw away at the vine.
The man saw a luscious strawberry near him.
Grasping the vine with one hand, he plucked
the strawberry with the other.
How sweet it tasted!

January 25

The great mistake in swordsmanship is to anticipate the outcome of the engagement; you ought not to be thinking of whether it ends in victory or defeat. Just let Nature take its course and your sword will strike at the right moment.

Zen never leaves this world of facts.
Zen always lives in the midst of
realities. It is not for Zen to stand apart
or keep itself away from a world of
names and forms.

January 27

This mind is the source, the Buddha,
absolutely pure in its nature, and it is present
in every one of us. All sentient beings,
however mean and degraded, are not in this
particular respect different from Buddhas
and *Bodhisattvas* – they are all of one
substance. Only because of their
imaginations and false discriminations,
sentient beings work out their *karma* and
reap its result while, in their Buddha-essence
itself, there is nothing corresponding to it:
the essence is empty and allows everything to
pass through – it is quiet and at rest,
it is illuminating, it is peaceful and
productive of bliss.

When, just as they are,
white dewdrops gather
on scarlet maple leaves,
regard the scarlet beads.

Small views are full of foxy fears;
the faster, the slower.
When we attach ourselves
to the idea of enlightenment,
we lose our balance;
we infallibly enter the crooked way.
When we are not attached to
anything, all things are as they are;
with Activity there is
no going or staying.
Obeying our nature,
we are in accord with the Way,
wandering freely, without annoyance.

January 30

One day Banzan was walking through a
market. He overheard a customer say
to the butcher, 'Give me the best piece of
meat you have.'
'Everything in my shop is the best,'
replied the butcher. 'You cannot find any
piece of meat that is not the best.'
At these words, Banzan was enlightened.

January 31

The breezes of spring
are blowing the ripples astray
along the water –
today they will surely melt
the sheet of ice on the pond.

February

February 1

*The cries of the insects
are buried at the roots
of sparse pampas grass –
the end of Autumn is in
the colour of the last leaves.*

February 2

A lord asked Takuan, a Zen teacher, to suggest how he might pass his time. He felt his days were very long when he was attending to his office and sitting stiffly to receive the homage of others.

Takuan wrote eight Chinese characters and gave them to the man:

> Not twice this day
> Inch time foot gem.

> This day will not come again.
> Each minute is worth a priceless gem.

February 3

High, high from the summit
of the peak,
whatever way I look, no limit in sight!
No one knows I am sitting here alone.
A solitary moon shines
in the cold spring.
Here in the spring –
this is not the moon.
The moon is where it always is –
in the sky above.
And, though I sing this one little song,
in the song there is no Zen.

February 4

*Walking is Zen, sitting is Zen,
whether talking or remaining silent,
whether moving or standing quiet,
the essence itself is ever at ease;
even when greeted with swords and
spears, it never loses its quiet way,
so with poisonous drugs, they fail to
perturb its serenity.*

February 5

You must concentrate on Zen practice
without wasting time, thinking that
there is only this day and this hour.
After that it becomes truly easy.
You must forget about the good or the
bad of your nature, the strength and
weakness of your power.

February 6

Gettan Osho said,
"Keichu, the first wheelmaker, made a cart
whose wheels
had a hundred spokes.
Now, suppose you took a cart and removed
both the wheels and the axle. What would
you have?"

Mumon's comment:
if anyone can directly master this topic, his
eye will be like a shooting star, his spirit like a
flash of lightning.

February 7

The first aim of sitting is to unify the mind. For the average person, whose mind is being pulled in many directions, sustained concentration is virtually impossible. Through the practice of *zazen*, the mind becomes one-pointed so that it can be controlled. The process can be likened to utilizing the sun's rays through a magnifying glass. When the rays of the sun are focused they become, of course, more intense. The human mind also functions more efficiently when it is concentrated and unified. Whether your desire is to see into your self-nature or not, you can appreciate the effect on your wellbeing or mind integration.

February 8

Our original nature is, in the highest truth, void, silent, pure; it is glorious and mysterious peaceful joy – and that is all. Enter deeply into it by awakening to it yourself. That which is before you is, in all its fullness, utterly complete.

February 9

The stars on the pond;
again the winter shower
ruffles the water.

February 10

I obtained not the least thing from unexcelled, complete awakening and for this reason it is called 'unexcelled, complete awakening'.

February 11

Mind, an unruffled pool.
A thunderbolt! My middle eye
shot wide, revealing – my ordinary self.

*If a person knows the Tathagata,
discerning nothing exists in him,
and knows all elements are extinct,
that man will swiftly become
a Buddha.*

February 13

*The perfect way knows
no difficulties
except that it refuses to
make preferences;
only when freed from hate
and love does
it reveal itself fully and
without disguise.*

February 14

If, at all times and in all places, we steadily keep our thoughts free from foolish desire, and act wisely on all occasions, then we are practising wisdom. One foolish notion is enough to shut off wisdom, while one wise thought will bring it forth again.

February 15

The human mind discriminates itself from the things that appear to be outside of itself without first realizing that it has first created these very things within its own mind. This has been going on from beginningless time, and the delusion has become firmly fixed within the mind, and even adheres things to themselves.

February 16

Tanzan and Ekido were once travelling
together down a muddy road. A heavy rain
was still falling.

Coming round a bend, they met a lovely girl
in a silk kimono and sash who was unable to
cross the intersection.

'Come on, girl,' said Tanzan at once. Lifting
her in his arms, he carried her over the mud.
Ekido did not speak again until that night,
when they reached a lodging temple. Then
he could no longer restrain himself. 'We
monks don't go near females,' he told Tanzan,
'especially not young and lovely ones. It is
dangerous. Why did you do that?'

'I left the girl there,' said Tanzan. 'Are you still
carrying her?'

February 17

*In the landscape of spring there is
neither high nor low;
the flowering branches grow naturally,
some long, some short.*

February 18

The mirror is clear and reflects anything that comes before it and yet an image sticks to the mirror. The Buddha-mind (the real, unborn mind) is ten thousand times more clear than a mirror and more inexpressibly marvellous. In its light all such thoughts vanish without trace. If you put your faith in this way of understanding, however strongly such thoughts may arise they do no harm.

February 19

For people, life is a succession of
graspings and attachments and then,
because of it, they assume the illusion
of pain and suffering.

February 20

Seeking the mind with the mind –
is not this the greatest of all mistakes?
Illusion produces rest and motion;
illumination destroys
liking and disliking.
All these pairs of opposites
are created by our own folly.
Dreams, delusions, flowers of air –
why are we so anxious to have them
in our grasp?
Profit and loss, right and wrong,
away with them once and for all!

*The mind like a mirror is brightly
illuminating and knows
no obstructions,
it penetrates the vast universe
to its minutest crevices;
all its contents, multitudinous in form,
are reflected in the mind,
which, shining like a perfect gem, has
no surface, nor an inside.*

February 22

With the evening breeze,
the water laps against
the heron's legs.

February 23

My hut in spring:
true, there is nothing in it –
there is everything.

February 24

If an eye never falls asleep,
all dreams will by themselves cease;
if the mind retains its absoluteness,
the ten thousand things are of
one suchness.

February 25

At the north window, icy draughts
whistle through the cracks,
at the south pond, wild geese
huddle in snowy reeds,
above, the mountain moon is
pinched thin with cold,
freezing clouds threaten to plunge
from the sky.
Buddhas might descend to this
world by the thousand,
they couldn't add or subtract
one thing.

February 26

There is here, not there.
Infinity is before our eyes.

February 27

One in all,
all in one –
if only this were realized,
no more worry about you
not being perfect.

February 28

Eaten by a cat!
Perhaps the cricket's widow
is bewailing that.

February 29

One moonlit night, the nun Chiyono
was carrying water in an old pail
bound with bamboo. The bamboo
broke and the bottom fell out
of the pail and, at that moment,
Chiyono was set free!

She wrote:
"no more water in the pail!
No more moon in the water!"

March

March 1

This is the barrier
where people come and people go
exchanging farewells;
for friends and strangers alike
this is the meeting barrier.

March 2

Why, it's but the motion of
eyes and brows!
And here I've been seeking it
far and wide.
Awakened at last, I find the moon
above the pines,
the river surging high.

March 3

*When the deep mystery of one
suchness is fathomed,
all of a sudden we forget the
external entanglements;
when ten thousand things are viewed
in their oneness,
we return to the origin and remain
where we have ever been.*

March 4

Infinitely small things are as
large as large things can be,
for here no external conditions obtain;
infinitely large things are as small as
small things can be,
for objective limits are here of
no consideration.

March 5

The morning glory
which blooms for an hour
differs not in heart from the giant pine,
which lives for a thousand years.

March 6

Nan-in, a Japanese master, received a
university professor, full of learning and
talk, who came to inquire about Zen.
Nan-in served tea. He filled the visitor's
cup and then kept pouring. The professor
watched the overflow until he could no
longer restrain himself.

'It is over-full. No more will go in.'

'Like this cup,' Nan-in said, 'you are full
of your own opinions and speculations.
How can I show you Zen unless you first
empty your cup?'

March 7

*When the deep mystery of one
suchness is fathomed,
all of a sudden we forget the
external entanglements;
when ten thousand things are viewed
in their oneness,
we return to the origin and remain
where we have ever been.*

March 8

Everything is mind-made and has no
significance apart from mind.
As people come to understand this fact,
they are able to remove all delusions
and there is an end to all mental
disturbances forever.

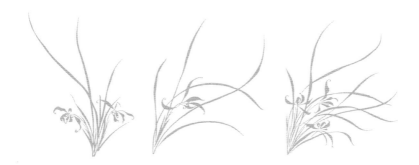

March 9

Mountains and plains,
all are taken by the snow —
nothing remains.

March 10

*In being 'not two' all is the same,
all that is comprehended in it;
the wise in the ten quarters,
they all enter into this
absolute reason.*

March 11

You may have most earnestly and diligently disciplined yourself for the past three *asamkhyeya kalpas* and passed through all the stages of *Bodhisattvahood*; but when you come to the realization in one thought, it is no other than this, that you are from the first the Buddha himself and no other.

Look upon the body as unreal,
an image in a mirror,
reflection of the moon in water.
Contemplate the mind as formless
yet bright and pure.

March 13

A monk asked Chimon,
'Before the lotus blossom has emerged from
the water, what is it?'
Chimon said, 'A lotus blossom'.
The monk pursued, 'After it has come out of
the water, what is it?'
Chimon replied, 'Lotus leaves'.
Shuzan held out his short staff and said,
'If you call this a short staff, you oppose
its reality because you are attached to its
name. If you do not call it a short staff,
you ignore the fact of it.
Now what do you want to call this?'

The comment:
Shuzan wants to know what this is.
It just is. Experience it.
Don't talk about it.

March 14

Like the empty sky
it has no boundaries,
yet it is right in this place,
ever profound and clear.
When you seek to know it,
you cannot see it.
You cannot take hold of it,
but you cannot lose it.
In not being able to get it, you get it.
When you are silent, it speaks;
When you speak, it is silent.
The great gate is open to bestow alms,
and no crowd is blocking the way.

March 15

*Energize your spirit
without becoming attached
to form or formlessness.*

March 16

Zen doctrine is no
subject for sentiment.
Doubts cannot be cleared by argument.
I stubbornly demand your silence
to save you from the pitfall of
being and non-being.

March 17

A dog and Buddha-nature?
The answer is in the question.
If you think of it in terms of duality,
you lose both body and life.

March 18

The ultimate end of things
is not bound by rules and measures;
In the mind harmonious we have the
principle of identity, in which we find
all strivings quieted;
doubts and irresolutions
are completely done away with,
and the right faith is straightened;
there is nothing retained;
all is void, lucid, and self-illuminating,
there is no waste of energy –
this is where thinking never attains,
this is where the imagination fails
to measure.

March 19

*On the moor: from things
detached completely —
how the skylark sings.*

March 20

Bodhidharma was received by the Emperor Wu, already a committed Buddhist, who was anxious to obtain approval from this renowned monk. He asked Bodhidharma:

'I have had temples built, holy scriptures copied and ordered monks and nuns to be converted. Is there any merit, Reverend Sir, in my conduct?'

'No merit at all.'

The Emperor was taken aback by this. It seemed that all he believed in was being turned upside down. He asked another question.

'What then is the holy truth, the first principle?'

'Vast emptiness with nothing holy in it.'

'Who then are you to stand before me?'

'I do not know, your Majesty.'

March 21

The thief
left it behind –
the moon at the window.

March 22

A monk came to a master and said, 'I have been here many years, but so far you have not imparted to me any Zen teaching. If this continues, I shall have to leave you.'
The master replied, 'In the morning when you salute me with, "Good morning!" I salute you with, "Good morning!" When you bring me a cup of tea, I gratefully drink it. When you do anything else for me, I acknowledge it. What other teachings do you want from me? There is no special teaching – the most ordinary things in our daily life hide some deep meaning that is yet most plain and explicit: only our eyes need to see where there is a meaning. Unless this eye is opened there will be nothing to learn from Zen.'

March 23

When we stop movement,
there is no-movement.
When we stop resting, there is no-rest.
When both cease to be,
how can the unity subsist?
Things are ultimately, in their finality,
subject to no law.
For the accordant mind in its unity,
individual activity ceases.
All doubts are cleared up,
true faith is confirmed.
Nothing remains behind;
there is not anything
we must remember.

March 24

What is, is not,
what is not, is.
Until you have grasped this fact,
your position is simply untenable.
One thing is all things;
all things are one thing.

March 25

Nothing whatever is hidden;
from of old, all is as clear as daylight.

March 26

The sun and the moon are always bright, yet if they are covered by clouds, although above they're bright, below they are darkened, and the sun, moon, stars and planets cannot be seen clearly. But if suddenly the wind of wisdom should blow and roll away the clouds and mists, all forms in the universe appear at once. The purity of the nature of man in this world is like the blue sky; wisdom is like the sun, knowledge like the moon. Although knowledge and wisdom are always clear, if you cling to external environments, the floating clouds of false thoughts will create a cover and your own natures cannot become clear.

March 27

In the dark forest
a berry drops:
the sound of water.

March 28

When the mind is like wood or stone,
there is nothing to be discriminated.

One stroke has made me forget
all of my previous knowledge,
no artificial discipline is needed;
in every movement
I uphold the ancient Way,
and never fall into the rut of quietism;
no traces are left where I walk
and my senses are not fettered
by rules of conduct;
everywhere all those who have
attained the truth,
declare this to be of the highest order.

March 30

A sudden light gleam:
off in the darkness goes
the night, the heron's scream.

March 31

Unfettered at last, a travelling monk,
I pass the old Zen barrier.
Mine is a traceless
stream-and-cloud life,
of these mountains,
which shall be my home?

April

April 1

Who would have thought that the essence of mind is intrinsically pure? Who would have thought that the essence of mind is intrinsically free from becoming and annihilation, is intrinsically self-sufficient, is intrinsically free from change? Who would have thought that all things are the manifestation of the essence of mind?

April 2

On Mount Wu-t'ai the clouds
are steaming rice;
before the ancient Buddha hall,
dogs piss at heaven.

Hini the herb grows on the Himalaya
where no other grasses are found,
and the cows feeding on it give the
purest of milk, and this I always enjoy.
One Nature, perfect and pervading,
circulates in all natures;
one Reality, all-comprehensive,
contains within itself all realities;
the one moon reflects itself wherever
there is a sheet of water,
and all the moons in the waters are
embraced within the one moon;
the Dharma-*body of all the Buddhas*
enters into my own being,
and my own being is found
in union with theirs.

April 4

This mind-essence is variously characterized as something original, mysterious, mysteriously bright, illuminating, true, perfect, clear as a jewel. It is not to be confused with our empirical mind, for it is not an object of thought.

April 5

*One word settles heaven and earth;
one sword levels the whole world.*

April 6

*Empty, lucid, self-illuminated,
with no over-exertion of the
power of the mind.
This is where thought is useless.
This is what knowledge cannot fathom.*

April 7

Wisdom does not vary with different persons; what makes the difference is whether one's mind is enlightened or deluded. He who does not know his own essence of mind and is under the illusion that Buddhahood can be attained by outward religious rites is called slow-witted.

April 8

Baso was once asked by a monk,
'What is Buddha?'
He replied, 'There is no mind,
no Buddha.'

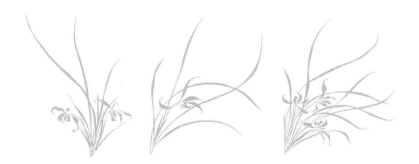

April 9

*In the dense mist,
what is being shouted
between hill and boat?*

*The morality-jewel inherent in the
Buddha-nature stamps itself on the
mind-ground of the enlightened one;
whose robe is cut out of mists, clouds,
and dews, whose bowl anciently
pacified the fiery dragons, and whose
staff once separated the fighting tigers;
listen now to the golden rings of his
staff giving out mellifluous tunes.
These are not mere symbolic expressions
devoid of historical contents;
wherever the holy staff of
Tathagatahood moves,
the traces are distinctly marked.*

April 11

When Ryonen was about to pass from this world, she wrote another poem:

Sixty-six times have these eyes beheld the changing scene of autumn, I have had enough about moonlight, ask no more, only listen to the voice of pines and cedars when no wind stirs.

April 12

Our original nature . . . is pure being, which is the source of everything and which appears as sentient beings or as Buddhas, as the rivers and mountains of the world which have form, as that which is formless or, as penetrating the whole universe, is absolutely without distinctions: there being no such entities as self and others.

April 13

*Perfect like Great Space
the Way has nothing lacking,
nothing in excess.
Truly, because of our accepting
and rejecting,
we have not the suchness of things.
Neither follow after,
nor dwell with the Doctrine
of the Void.
If the mind is at peace,
these wrong views disappear
of themselves.*

April 14

There is no place to seek the mind;
it is like the footprints of the birds
in the sky.

April 15

He neither seeks the true nor
severs himself from the defiled,
he clearly perceives that dualities
are empty and have no reality,
that to have no reality means not
to be one-sided, neither empty
nor not-empty,
for this is the genuine form
of Tathagatahood.

April 16

Winter desolation;
in the rainwater tub,
sparrows are walking.

April 17

A Zen master named Gisan asked a young
student to bring him a pail of water to cool
his bath.
The student brought the water and, after
cooling the bath, threw on to the ground the
little that was left over.
'You dunce!' the master scolded him. 'Why
didn't you give the water to the plants? What
right have you to waste even a drop of water
in this temple?'
The young student attained Zen in that
instant. He changed his name to Tekisui,
which means a drop of water.

April 18

Body clothed in no-cloth robe,
feet clad in turtle's fur boots,
I seize my bow of rabbit horn
and prepare to shoot the
devil ignorance.

April 19

In nothingness of man I delight,
and of all being,
a thousand worlds complete in
my little cage.
I forget sin, demolish my heart,
and in enlightenment rejoice;
who tells me that the fallen
suffer in Hell's bonds?

April 20

Fathomed at last!
Ocean's dried. Void burst.
Without an obstacle in sight,
it's everywhere!

The essence is there,
is evident from the fact
that the eye sees, the ear hears
and the mind thinks.
Only it is not discoverable
as an individual object or idea,
objectice or subjective
for it has no existence in the way
we talk of a tree or a sun
of a virtue or a thought.

April 22

A long thing is the long body of the Buddha.
A short thing is the short body of the Buddha.

April 23

True emptiness – that which is beyond concepts and words – is sometimes called 'suchness' or 'thusness'. It means 'it is so'. It can only be directly experienced. If you want to know what an orange is like, you have to taste it. Then you enter the suchness of an orange or the suchness of the sea. In Zen, the very beginningness of our life is its suchness. To know that beginningness, you must experience it without concepts.

April 24

What is the same as what is not,
what is not is the same as what is:
where this state of things
fails to obtain,
indeed, no tarrying there.

April 25

There is no reality even prior
to Heaven and Earth;
indeed, it has no form,
much less a name;
eyes fail to see it;
it has no voice for ears to detect;
to call it Mind or Buddha
violates its nature,
for it then becomes a visionary
flower in the air;
it is not Mind nor Buddha.

April 26

When the nun Chiyono studied Zen under
Bukko of Engaku she was unable to obtain
the fruits of meditation for a long time.
At last, one moonlit night, she was carrying
water in an old pail bound with bamboo. The
bamboo broke and the bottom fell out of the
pail: at that moment, Chiyono was set free!
In commemoration, she wrote a poem:

In this way and that,
I tried to save the old pail
since the bamboo strip was weakening
and about to break
until at last the bottom fell out,
no more water in the pail!
No more moon in the water!

April 27

Learned audience, those who recite the word 'wisdom' the whole day long do not seem to know that wisdom is inherent in their own nature. But mere talking of food will not appease hunger and this is exactly the case with these people.

April 28

*A fallen flower
returning to the branch?
It was a butterfly.*

April 29

What we have to do is to purify our mind so that the six *Vijnanas* (aspects of consciousness), in passing through the six gates (sense organs), will neither be defiled by, nor attached to, the six sense-objects. When our mind works freely without hindrance, and is at liberty to 'come' and 'go', we attain *Samadhi* or *prajna* (liberation). Such a state is called the function of 'thoughtlessness'. But to refrain from thinking of anything, so that all thoughts are suppressed, is to be *Dharma*-ridden and is an erroneous view.

April 30

Because we are running after objects, we lose track of the original mind and are tormented by the threatening objective world, regarding it as good or bad, true or false, agreeable or disagreeable. We are thus slaves of things and circumstances. The Buddha advises that our real position ought to be exactly the opposite.

Let things follow us and await our commands. Let the true self give directions in all of our dealings with the world.

May

May 1

If you fail to achieve emancipation in this
life, when do you expect to achieve it?
While still alive you should be tireless in
practising contemplation. The practice
consists of abandonments. 'The
abandonment of what?', you may ask. You
should abandon all the workings of your
relative consciousness, which you have been
cherishing since eternity; retire within your
inner being and see the reason of it. As
yourself-reflection grows deeper and deeper,
the moment will surely come upon you when
the spiritual flower will suddenly burst into
bloom, illuminating the entire universe.

May 2

Leaves falling,
lie on one another;
the rain beats on the rain.

May 3

Like a sword that cuts,
but cannot cut itself;
like an eye, but cannot see itself.

May 4

Ikkyu, the Zen master, was very clever even as a boy. His teacher had a precious teacup, a rare antique. Ikkyu happened to break this cup and was greatly perplexed. Hearing the footsteps of his teacher, he held the pieces of the cup behind him. When the master appeared, Ikkyu asked: 'Why do people have to die?'

'This is natural,' explained the older man. 'Everything has to die and has just so long to live.'

Ikkyu, producing the shattered cup, added: 'It was time for your cup to die.'

May 5

Though numbers of sutras be plundered of their contents, success will never be attained. By looking into inner understanding, enlightenment will be realized in a flash of thought.

May 6

Human mind on its highest level is universal mind. As universal mind, it is pure, tranquil, unconditioned, in its true essential nature, but because of its relations with the lower minds it becomes the storage for their reactions.

May 7

Master Sessan said: 'The secret of seeing things as they are is to take off our coloured spectacles. That being-as-it-is, with nothing extraordinary about it, nothing wonderful, is the great wonder. The ability to see things normally is no small thing; to be really normal is unusual. In that normality inspiration begins to bubble up.'

May 8

If you don't believe, just look at
September, look at October!
The yellow leaves falling, falling,
to fill both mountain and river.

Finding that none of you would understand, the Buddhas gave it the name *Tao*, but you must not base any concept on that name. So it is said that 'when the fish is caught the trap is forgotten'.

May 10

If the essence is anything of which we can make any statements, either affirmative or negative, it is no more the essence. It is independent of all forms and ideas, and yet we cannot speak of it as not dependent on them. It is absolute emptiness, sunyata, *and for this very reason, all things are possible in it.*

May 11

*To bird and butterfly
it is unknown, this flower here:
the autumn sky.*

May 12

A *sutra* says: 'It is only a group of elements that come together to create a body. When it arises, only these elements arise. When it ceases only these elements cease. But when the elements arise do not say, "I am arising", and when they cease do not say, "I am ceasing". So, too, with our former thoughts, later thoughts and intervening thoughts: the thoughts follow one another without being linked together. Each one is absolutely tranquil.'

May 13

Gasan instructed his adherents one day: 'Those who speak against killing and desire to spare the lives of all conscious beings are right. It is good to protect even animals and insects. But what about those persons who kill time, what about those who are destroying wealth and those who destroy political economy? We should not overlook them. Furthermore, what of the one who preaches without enlightenment? He is killing Buddhism.'

May 14

Better emancipate your mind
than your body;
when the mind is emancipated,
the body is free,
when both body and mind
are emancipated,
even gods and spirits ignore
worldly power.

May 15

The sea darkens;
The voices of the wild ducks
Are faintly white.

May 16

If we watch the shore while we are sailing in a boat, we feel that the shore is moving. But if we look nearer to the boat itself, we know then that it is the boat that moves. When we regard the universe in confusion of body and mind, we often get the mistaken belief that our mind is constant. But if we actually practise Zen and come back to ourselves, we see that this was wrong.

May 17

'I have no peace of mind,' said Hui-k'o.
'Please pacify my mind.'
' Bring out your mind here before me,'
replied Bodhidharma, 'and I will pacify it.'
'But when I seek my own mind,' said Hui-k'o,
'I cannot find it.'
'There!' snapped Bodhidharma,
'I have pacified your mind.'

May 18

Men are afraid to lose their own minds, fearing to fall through the void with nothing to which they can cling. They do not know that the void is not really the void, but the realm of *Dharma* . . . It cannot be looked for or sought, comprehended by wisdom or knowledge, explained in words, contacted materially [objectively] or reached by meritorious achievement.

May 19

A monk said to Joshu, 'I have just entered this monastery. Please teach me.'
'Have you eaten your rice porridge?' asked Joshu.
'Yes, I have,' replied the monk.
'Then you had better wash your bowl,' said Joshu.
With this the monk gained insight.

Mumon's comment
When he opens his mouth, Joshu shows his gall bladder. He displays his heart and liver.
I wonder if this monk really did hear the truth?
I hope he did not mistake the bell for a jar.

Mumon's verse
Endeavouring to interpret clearly,
You retard your attainment.
Don't you know that flame is fire?
Your rice has long been cooked.

May 20

*If for one instant of thought
we become impartial,
then sentient beings are
themselves Buddha.
In our mind itself a Buddha exists,
our own Buddha is the true Buddha.*

May 21

In the world of reality,
there is no self, no other-than-self.
Should you desire immediate
correspondence [with this reality]
all that can be said is 'no duality!'

May 22

The illimitable void of the universe is capable of
holding myriads of things of various shapes and
forms, such as the sun, the moon, the stars,
mountains, rivers, worlds, springs, rivulets, bushes,
woods, good men, bad men, *Dharmas* pertaining
to goodness or badness, Deva planes, hells, great
oceans and all the mountains of Mahameru.
Space takes in all of these and so does the
voidness of nature. We say the essence of mind is
great because it embraces all things, since all
things are within our nature.

May 23

When thoughts are not sound,
the spirit is troubled;
what is the point of being partial
and one-sided then?
If you want to walk the course
of the One Vehicle,
be not prejudiced against the
six sense-objects.

May 24

Abide not with dualism,
carefully avoid pursuing it;
as soon as you have right and wrong,
confusion ensues and mind is lost.

May 25

*The wild geese do not intend
to cast their reflection;
the water has no mind to
receive their image.*

May 26

The two exist because of the one,
but hold not even to this one;
when a mind is not disturbed,
the ten thousand things
offer no offence.

Things which are past are past.
Do not speculate about them.
When your mind cuts itself off from
the past, that is called having no past.
Future events have not taken place.
Do not desire to seek for them.
When your mind cuts itself off from
the future that is called having no
future. Present events are present.

May 28

How admirable,
he who thinks not, 'Life is fleeting',
when he sees the lightning!

May 29

This absolute reason is beyond
quickening [time] and
extending [space],
for if one instant is
ten thousand years;
whether we see it or not,
it is manifest everywhere in all
the ten quarters.

May 30

*There is nothing difficult about the
Great Way, but, avoid choosing!
Only when you neither love nor hate,
does it appear in all clarity.
A hair's breadth of deviation from it,
and a deep gulf is set
between heaven and earth.
If you want to get hold
of what it looks like,
do not be for or against anything.
The conflict of longing and loathing –
this is the disease of the mind.
Not knowing the
profound meaning of things,
we disturb our original peace of mind
to no purpose.*

May 31

Above, below and around you, all is spontaneously existing, for there is nowhere which is outside the mind.

June

June 1

'Thought' means thinking of the original nature of True Reality. True Reality is the substance of thoughts; thoughts are the function of True Reality. If you give rise to thoughts from your self-nature then, although you see, hear, perceive, and know, you are not stained by the manifold environments and are always free.
The *Vimalakirti Sutra* says: 'Externally, while distinguishing well all the forms of the various dharmas, internally he stands firm within the First Principle.'

June 2

Just as a peaceful ocean becomes suddenly a tumult of waves because of some passing tempest, so the ocean of mind becomes stirred by tempests of delusion and the winds of *karma*.

June 3

You must clearly understand that this
Way is the void which depends on
nothing and is attached to nothing.
It is all-pervading, spotless beauty; it is
self-existent and uncreated Absolute.

June 4

A brushwood gate,
and for a lock —
this snail.

June 5

A new student approached the Zen master and asked how he should prepare himself for his training. 'Think of me as a bell,' the master explained. 'Give me a soft tap, and you will get a tiny ping. Strike hard, and you'll receive a loud, resounding peal.'

June 6

All these existences and conditions take place illusively in the mind-essence. It is this alone that eternally abides as suchness: bright, illuminating, all-pervading and immovable. In this essence of eternal truth, there is indeed neither coming nor going, neither becoming confused nor being enlightened, neither dying nor being born. It is absolutely unattainable and unexplainable by the intellect for it lies beyond all the categories of thought.

June 7

Entering the forest
he moves not the grass.
Entering the water
he makes not a ripple.

The Way is perfect like
unto vast space,
with nothing wanting,
nothing superfluous;
it is indeed due to making a choice
that its suchness is lost sight of.

June 9

A rich man asked Sengai to write something for the continued prosperity of his family. Sengai obtained a large sheet of paper and wrote: 'Father dies, son dies, grandson dies'. The rich man became angry. 'I asked you to write something for the happiness of my family! Why do you make such a joke of this?' 'No joke is intended,' explained Sengai. 'If before you yourself die your son should die, this would grieve you greatly. If your grandson should pass away before your son both of you would be broken-hearted. If your family, generation after generation, passes away in the order I have named, it will be the natural course of life. I call this real prosperity.'

June 10

Just as the ocean becomes peaceful
when the tempest passes, so the ocean
of mind resumes its natural calm when
the winds of *karma* are stilled.

June 11

There is no place in Buddhism for using effort. Just be ordinary and nothing special. Relieve your bowels, pass water, put on your clothes and eat your food. When you are tired go and lie down. Ignorant people may laugh at me, but the wise will understand.

June 12

The breezes of spring
are blowing the ripples astray
along the water –
today they will surely melt
the sheet of ice on the pond.

June 13

Po-cheng had so many students that he had
to open a second monastery. To find a
suitable person as its master, he called his
monks together and set a pitcher before them.
'Without calling it a pitcher, tell me what it is.'
The head monk said, 'You couldn't call it a
piece of wood.'
At this the monastery cook kicked the pitcher
over and walked away. The cook was put in
charge of the new monastery.

June 14

*In the landscape of spring there is
neither high nor low;
the flowering branches grow naturally,
some long, some short.*

June 15

There's nothing equal to wearing clothes and eating food.

June 16

There I was, hunched over
my office desk,
mind an unruffled pool.
A thunderbolt! My middle eye
shot wide, revealing –
my ordinary self.

June 17

Ryokan, a Zen master, lived the simplest kind of life in a little hut at the foot of a mountain. One evening a thief visited the hut only to discover that there was nothing in it to steal. Ryokan returned and caught him. 'You may have come a long way to visit me,' he told the prowler, 'and you should not return empty-handed. Please take my clothes as a gift.'

The thief was bewildered. He took the clothes and slunk away.

Ryokan sat naked watching the moon.

'Poor fellow,' he mused, 'I wish I could give him this beautiful moon.'

June 18

I lay sick by the low window,
propped on a crooked bed,
and thought how orderly
the universe is.
A white bird flew across the sky;
and my mind rolled forth ten
thousand feet.

June 19

Just as the ocean becomes peaceful when the tempest passes, so the ocean of mind resumes its natural calm when the winds of *karma* are stilled.

June 20

The mind that creates its surroundings is never free from their shadow; it remembers, fears and laments, not only the past but the present and the future because they have arisen out of ignorance and greed. It is out of ignorance and greed that the world of delusion starts and the vast complex of co-ordinating causes and conditions exist within the mind and nowhere else.

June 21

The mind-essence is in itself thoroughly pure and all-pervading, and in it this formula holds: form is emptiness and emptiness is form. Rupam sunyata, sunyateva rupam.

June 22

Very soon they die —
but of that there is no sign
in the locust-cry.

June 23

Yamaoka Tsshu, as a young student of Zen, visited one master after another. He called upon Dokuon of Shokoku.

Desiring to show his attainment, he said: 'The mind, Buddha, and sentient beings, after all, do not exist. The true nature of phenomena is emptiness. There is no realization, no delusion, no sage, no mediocrity. There is no giving and nothing to be received.'

Dokuon, who was smoking quietly, said nothing. Suddenly he whacked Yamaoka with his bamboo pipe. This made the youth quite angry.

'If nothing exists,' inquired Dokuon, 'where did this anger come from?'

June 24

O my good friends gathered here,
if you desire to listen to the
thunderous voice of the Way,
exhaust your words,
empty your thoughts,
for then you may come to
recognize this one essence.

This mind-essence reveals itself in accordance with the thoughts and dispositions of all beings, in response to their infinitely varied degrees of knowledge, and also to their karma. *In spite of its being involved in the evolution of a world of multiplicities, the essence in itself never loses its original purity, the brilliance or emptiness.*

June 26

Above, below and around you all is spontaneously existing, for there is nowhere which is outside the mind.

June 27

*Direct your eye right inward,
and you'll find
a thousand regions of your mind
yet undiscovered. Travel them and be
expert in home-cosmography.*

June 28

All *sutras* and Scriptures of the Mahayana and Hinayana Schools, as well as the twelve sections of the canonical writings, were provided to suit different needs and the different temperaments of various people.
It is upon the principle that wisdom is latent in every man that the doctrines expounded in these books are established.

June 29

*The steam hides itself
in the grasses
of departing Autumn.*

June 30

In Zen, one would say that the completely enlightened being no longer rests on any external moral code, but naturally does good and refrains from doing evil, out of the very depth of the heart.

July

July 1

This mind is no mind of
conceptual thought and it is
completely detached from form, so
Buddhas and sentient beings do not
differ at all. If you can only rid
yourselves of conceptual thought you
will accomplish everything.

July 2

Meditation is practised in four ways. First, your mind and body are still. This is the source of all your Zen actions. Second, your body is still but your mind moves, as in reading or listening to a lecture. Third, your mind is still but your body moves, as in walking. Fourth, your mind and body move as you do your work in daily life. Thus, each moment, a good Zen student experiences the mind-essence ever at ease.

July 3

*To see the truth here is the end
of Zen study.
Give a sword to a fencing-master,
do not give a poem to a man
who is not a poet.
In conversation reveal one third,
never give out the whole.*

July 4

I have locked the gate on a
thousand peaks
to live here with clouds and birds.
All day I watch the hills
as clear winds fill the bamboo door.
A supper of pine flowers,
monk's robes of chestnut dye —
what dream does the world hold
to lure me from these dark slopes?

July 5

The Three Thousand Worlds
that step forward
with the light snow,
and the light snow that falls
in those Three Thousand Worlds.

July 6

In former times men's minds were sharp. Upon hearing a single sentence, they abandoned study and so came to be called 'the sages who, abandoning learning, rest in spontaneity'. In these days, people only seek to stuff themselves with knowledge and deductions, placing great reliance on written explanations and calling all this the practice.

July 7

Mind is like the void in which there is
no confusion or evil, as when the sun
wheels through it shining upon the
four corners of the world. For when
the sun rises and illuminates the whole
earth the void gains not in brilliance;
and when the sun sets the void
does not darken.

July 8

The realization of one mind may come after a shorter or a longer period. There are those who, upon hearing this teaching, rid themselves of conceptual thought in a flash. There are those who do this after following the Ten Beliefs, the Ten Stages, the Ten Activities and the Ten Bestowals of Merit. Yet others accomplish it through the Ten Stages of the *Bodhisattva's* Progress. But whether they transcend conceptual thought by a longer or a shorter way, the result is a state of being; there is no pious practising and no action of realizing.

July 9

Refreshing, the wind against the wind
against the waterfall
as the moon hangs, a lantern
on the peak
and the bamboo window glows.
In old age mountains
are more beautiful than ever.
My resolve:
that these bones be purified by rocks.

July 10

The deluded person concentrates on Buddha and wishes to be born in the other land; the awakened person makes pure his own mind. Therefore the Buddha said: 'In accordance with the purity of the mind the Buddha-land is pure.'

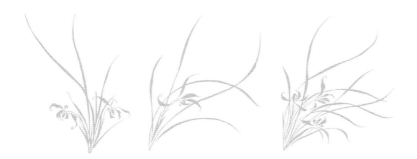

July 11

*Truth cannot be increased or decreased;
an instantaneous thought lasts
a myriad years.
There is no here, no there;
infinity is before our eyes.*

July 12

*If the eye does not sleep,
all dreaming ceases naturally.
If the mind makes no discriminations,
all things are as they really are.*

July 13

Not a mote in the light above,
soul itself cannot offer such a view.
Though dawn's not come,
the cock is calling:
the phoenix, flower in beak,
welcomes spring.

July 14

Infinitely small things are as large as
large things can be,
for here no external conditions obtain;
infinitely large things are as small
as small things can be,
for objective limits are here
of no consideration.

July 15

Do not seek for the truth;
religiously avoid following it.
If there is the slightest trace
of this and that,
the mind is lost in a maze
of complexity.
Duality arises from unity –
but do not be attached to this unity.

July 16

The wise man does nothing;
the fool shackles himself.
The truth has no distinctions;
these come from our foolish clinging
to this and that.

July 17

*Deluded, a Buddha is a sentient being;
awakened, a sentient being
is a Buddha.
Ignorant, a Buddha is a sentient being;
with wisdom, a sentient being
is a Buddha.*

July 18

For long years, a bird in a cage;
today, flying along with clouds.

July 19

With the lamp of word and discrimination one must go beyond the word and discrimination and enter upon the path of realization.

July 20

As you go from place to place, if you regard each one as your home, they will all be genuine, for when circumstances come, you must not try to change them. Thus your usual habits of feeling, which make *karma* for Five Hells, will of themselves become the Great Ocean of Liberation.

July 21

Like lightning it flashes through the shadows, severing the spring wind; the God of Nothingness bleeds crimson streaming.
I tremble at the heights of Mount Sumera;
I will dive, I will leap into the stem of a lotus.

July 22

You have always been at one with Buddha, so do not pretend you can attain to oneness by various practices.

July 23

When you hear me talking of the void, do not at once fall into the idea of vacuity. It is of the utmost importance that we should not fall into this idea, because when a man sits quietly and keeps his mind blank, he will reside in a state of 'voidness of indifference'.

July 24

Daiju visited Master Baso in China. Baso
asked: 'What do you seek?'
'Enlightenment', replied Daiju.
'You have your own treasure house.
Why do you search outside?' Baso asked.
Daiju enquired: 'Where is my treasure house?'
Baso answered: 'What you are asking is your
treasure house.'
Daiju was enlightened! Ever after he urged
his friends: 'Open your treasure house and
use those treasures.'

*There is neither self nor living beings;
also there is no defeat or ruin;
whoever obtains such knowledge as this
will accomplish supreme
enlightenment.*

July 26

To keep our minds free from defilement under all circumstances is called 'idea-lessness'. Our mind should stand aloof from circumstances and by no account should we allow them to influence the function of our mind. But it is a great mistake to suppress our mind from all thinking; for even if we succeed in getting rid of all thoughts, and die immediately thereafter, we shall be reincarnated elsewhere.

July 27

I ask whether Zen can be used by artists, as it might have been by the great master Sesshu, to achieve the proper state of mind for serious artistic production. The master's answer was, 'Zen is not something to be "used"; Zen art is nothing more than an expression of Zen spirit.'

July 28

The body and its surroundings are all alike manifestations of the one mind, but as observed by the human eye they appear to be different and they are classified as 'observer' and as 'things observed'. But as nothing exists apart from mind, there can be no essential difference between subject and object.

July 29

To a monk departing on a trading
mission to China:

To judge for yourself whether the
weather be hot or cold;
A fellow must not be cheated by others.
And see that you take not Japan's
good gold
And barter it off for Chinese brass!

July 30

It is told again by the Tathagata that this *Dharma* is perfectly even and free from irregularities. By *Dharma* is meant *Bodhi*. That is, this pure mind forming the source of all things is perfectly even in all sentient beings, in all the Buddha lands, and also in all the other worlds together with mountains, oceans, etc., things with form and things without form. They are all even and there are no marks of distinction between this object and that. This pure mind, the source of all things, is always perfect and illuminating and all-pervading.

July 31

If they put a stop to conceptual thought and forget their anxiety, the Buddha will appear before them, for this mind is the Buddha and the Buddha is all living beings. It is not the less for being manifested in ordinary beings, nor is it greater for being manifested as the Buddha.

247

August

August 1

When thoughts arise, then do all things arise. When thoughts vanish, then do all things vanish.

August 2

My advice to those whose eyes
have not been opened to the truth –
leap from the net and see how
immense is the ocean.

August 3

There is only one reality, neither to be realized or attained. To say 'I am able to realize something' or 'I am able to attain something' is to place yourself among the arrogant.

August 4

Regarding all things, only understand
that there must be no attachment.
No attachment means that feelings of
hatred and love do not arise.

To train yourself in sitting meditation (*zazen*) is to train yourself to be a sitting Buddha. If you train yourself in *zazen* (you should know that) Zen is never sitting nor lying. If you train yourself to be a sitting Buddha (you should know that) the Buddha is not a fixed form.

August 6

*Wind subsiding,
the flowers still fall;
bird crying, the mountain
silence deepens.*

August 7

This is the reason why the swordsman is always advised to be free from the thought of death or from anxiety about the outcome of the combat. As long as there is any 'thought' of whatever nature, that will assuredly prove disastrous.

August 8

While Zen teaching consists in grasping the spirit by transcending form, it unfailingly reminds us of the fact that the spirit expresses itself only by means of form.

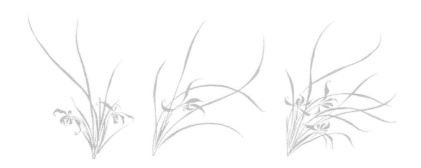

August 9

When the followers of Zen fail to go beyond a world of their senses and thoughts, all their doings and movements are of no significance. But when the senses and thoughts are annihilated, all the passages to the mind are blocked and no entrance then becomes possible. The original mind is to be recognized along with the working of the senses and thoughts; only it does not belong to them, nor is it independent of them.

August 10

On a withered branch
the crow is perched
in the autumn evening.

August 11

When activity is stopped
and passivity obtains,
this passivity again is
a state of activity.
Remaining in movement
or quiescence –
how shall we know the One?
Not thoroughly understanding
the unity of the Way,
both activity and quiescence
are failures.
If you get rid of phenomena,
all things are lost.
If you follow after the void, you turn
your back on the selflessness of things.

August 12

The infinitely small is as large
as the infinitely great;
for limits are non-existent things.
The infinitely large is as small
as the infinitely minute;
no eye can see their boundaries.

August 13

Things are things because
of the mind;
the mind is the mind
because of things.
If you wish to know what
these two are,
they are originally one emptiness.
In this void both [mind
and things] are one,
all the myriad phenomena
contained in both.

August 14

The tree is stripped,
all colour, fragrance gone,
yet already on the bough,
uncaring spring!

August 15

Master Ganto said to his brother:
'Whatever the great masters of Zen say,
however they expound their teachings, of
what use is all their learning and
understanding to another person? That
which gushes out from your own heart –
that is what embraces heaven and earth.'

August 16

That the self advances
and confirms the myriad things
is delusion.
That the myriad things advance
and confirm the self
is enlightenment.

Blue mountains are of themselves blue mountains; white clouds are of themselves white clouds.

August 18

Though many may talk of the Way of the Buddhas as something to be reached by various pious practices and by study, you must have nothing to do with such ideas. A perception, sudden as blinking, that subject and object are one, will lead to a deeply mysterious wordless understanding; and by this understanding you will awaken to the truth of Zen.

August 19

The sound of scouring
of the saucepan blends
with the tree frogs' voices.

August 20

A monk said to Shifukyu, 'I have not finished even one summer seclusion in the monastery, and I do not ask for your teaching – but help me please!'

Shifukyu pushed him away and said: 'Since I have been living here, I have never once blinded a monk. I have blinded many people with my explanations. I am still at it.'

If the mind is warped, a Buddha
is a sentient being;
if the mind is impartial, a sentient
being is a Buddha.
When once a warped mind is produced,
Buddha is concealed within
the sentient being.

August 22

A monk asked Tozan, 'How can we escape the cold and the heat?'
Tozan replied, 'Why not go where there is no cold and no heat?'
'Is there such a place?' the monk asked.
Tozan commented, 'When cold, be thoroughly cold; when hot, be hot through and through.'

August 23

When we use wisdom for introspection,
we are illumined within and without and in a
position to know our own mind. To know
our mind is to obtain liberation. To obtain
liberation is to obtain *Samadhi* of *prajna*,
which is 'thoughtlessness'. What is
'thoughtlessness'? Thoughtlessness is to see
all things with a mind free from attachment.
When in use it pervades everywhere and yet
sticks nowhere.

To study the Way is to study the self.
To study the self is to forget the self.
To forget the self is to be enlightened
by all things.
To be enlightened by all things
is to remove the barriers
between oneself and others.

August 25

*A village where they ring
no bells – oh what do they do
at dusk in spring?*

August 26

Do not keep perceptions nor abandon them nor cleave to them. Above, below and around you, all is spontaneous existing, for there is nowhere which is outside the Buddha-mind.

August 27

There a beggar goes!
Heaven and Earth he's wearing
for his summer clothes!

August 28

To a Korean friend:

The old man of the village
called us back
to drink three cups
beneath the crooked mulberry.
Mankind is small
but this drunkenness is wide and great –
where now Japan, where is your Korea?

August 29

Unmon said: 'I do not ask you about fifteen days ago. But what about fifteen days hence? Come, say a word about this!' Since none of the monks answered, he answered for them: 'Every day is a good day.'

August 30

A monk asked Kegon,
'How does an enlightened one
return to the ordinary world?'
Kegon replied, 'A broken mirror never
reflects again; fallen flowers never go
back to the old branches.'

August 31

If we do not have in ourselves
the Buddha mind,
then where are we to seek Buddha?

September

September 1

Here one sees neither sin nor bliss,
neither loss nor gain;
in the midst of the eternally serene
no idle questionings are invited;
the dust of ignorance has been since
days of old accumulating on
the mirror never polished,
now is the time once and for all to see
the cleaning positively done.

September 2

Clinging is never kept within bounds,
The Way calm and easy,
and free from annoyance;
but when your thoughts are tied,
you turn away from the truth,
they grow heavier and duller,
and are not at all sound.

September 3

When we return to the root,
we gain the meaning;
when we pursue external objects
we lose reason.
The moment we are
enlightened within,
we go beyond the voidness of
a world confronting us.

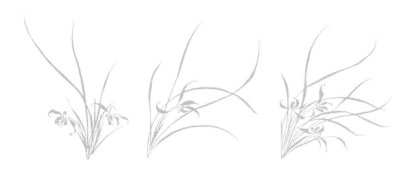

September 4

The activities of the mind have
no limit and form the surroundings of
life. An impure mind surrounds itself
with impure things and a pure mind
surrounds itself with pure
surroundings, hence surroundings
have no more limits than the activities
of the mind.

September 5

*No offence is offered, and
no ten thousand things;
no disturbance going, and no
mind set up to work;
the subject is quieted when
the object ceases,
the object ceases when the
subject is quieted.*

September 6

The mind is the Buddha, nor
are there any other Buddhas or any
other mind. It is bright and spotless as
the void, having no form or
appearance whatever.

September 7

Just as a peaceful ocean suddenly becomes a tumult of waves because of some passing tempest, so the ocean of mind becomes stirred by tempests of delusion and the winds of *karma*.

There is nothing in the world that is not mind-created and just as the human mind creates, the Buddha creates, and all other beings act as Buddha acts. So in the great task of creation the human mind, Buddha and all other beings are active alike.

September 9

It is doubt and unbelief that cause one to return over and over again to the House of Birth and Death; but through faith we enter into the peace of the Eternal City called *Nirvana.*

September 10

Nansen was once asked by Jyoshu,
'What is *Tao*?'
Nansen: 'Ordinary mind is *Tao*.'
Jyoshu: 'Should we try to get it?'
Nansen: 'As soon as you try you miss it.'
Jyoshu: 'How do we know without trying?'
Nansen: '*Tao* is beyond both knowing and
not knowing. Knowing is false perception
and not knowing is lack of awareness.
When one attains to *Tao* it is certain that one
will see it clearly as one sees the vastness of
the universe. Then what is the use of arguing
about it?'
At these words, Jyoshu was
suddenly enlightened.

September 11

A philosopher asked Buddha: 'Without words, without silence, will you tell me the truth?' The Buddha sat quietly. The philosopher then bowed and thanked the Buddha, saying, 'With your loving kindness I have cleared away my delusions and entered the true path.'

After the philosopher had gone, Ananda asked Buddha what the philosopher had attained. The Buddha commented, 'A good horse runs even at the shadow of the whip.'

September 12

*The object is an object for the subject,
the subject is a subject for the object;
know that the relativity of the two
rests ultimately on one emptiness.*

September 13

It has been the tradition of our school to take 'idea-lessness' as our object, 'non-objectivity' as our basis, and 'non-attachment' as our fundamental principle. 'Non-objectivity' means not to be absorbed by objects when in contact with objects. 'Idea-lessness' means not to be carried away by any particular idea in the exercise of the mental faculty. 'Non-attachment' is the characteristic of our essence of mind.

September 14

To us, Gautama and Amida appear like a father and mother, full of compassion. That we may embrace the priceless faith, they have taken many and various means to attract and persuade us.

September 15

*Transformation going on in an empty
world which confronts us
appear real all because of ignorance:
try not to seek after the true,
only cease to cherish opinions.*

September 16

The ever-existent Buddha is not a Buddha of stages. Only awake to the one mind, and there is nothing whatsoever to be attained. This is the *real* Buddha, and all sentient beings are the one mind and nothing else.

September 17

Hundreds of flowers in Spring
and the moon in Autumn,
cool breeze in Summer
and snow in Winter:
every season is a good season for you
unless you cherish an idle thought in
your mind.

September 18

A mind to search elsewhere
for the Buddha
is foolishness
in the very centre of foolishness.

September 19

My self of long ago,
in Nature non-existent;
nowhere to go when dead,
nothing at all.

September 20

Dogen was once asked, 'What is Zen?'.
His reply was, 'If you build a fence
around it there will be nothing inside.'

September 21

Man is born many times,
so he dies many times.
Life and death continue endlessly.
If he realizes the true meaning
of unborn,
he will transcend both gladness
and grief.

September 22

There is only one mind and not a particle of anything else on which to lay hold, for this mind is the Buddha. If you students of the Way do not awaken to this mind substance you will overlay mind with conceptual thought, you will seek the Buddha outside yourself and you will remain attached to forms.

He lives in equanimity calmly
and contentedly. He is free
from all care, yet he acts
naturally and reasonably.

He neither strives to avoid delusion nor
seeks after truth. He knows delusions
as baseless and truth as himself.

*Whoever can look at this earthly realm
in every aspect without attachment,
and likewise the Tathagat's body
this man will swiftly
achieve Buddhahood.*

September 25

Since early years I have sought eagerly after
scholarly attainment,
I have studied the sutras and sastras and
commentaries,
I have been given up to the analysis of names
and forms, and never known fatigue;
but diving into the ocean to count up its sands
is surely an exhausting task and a vain one;
the Buddha has never spared such, his
scoldings are just to the point,
for what is the use of reckoning the treasures
that are not mine?
All my past achievements have been efforts
vainly and wrongly applied – I realize now,
I have been a vagrant monk for many years to
no end whatever.

September 26

Emperor: 'Gudo, what happens to the man of enlightenment and the man of illusion after death?'
Gudo: 'How should I know, Sir?'
Emperor: 'Because you're a master.'
Gudo: 'Yes, sir, but not a dead one!'

September 27

If all things are to be returned
to the one, to where is that
one to be returned?

*Those who, reflecting
within themselves,
testify to the truth of self-nature,
to the truth that self-nature
is no nature,
have gone beyond all sophistry.
For them opens the gate of oneness
of cause and effect,
and straight runs the path of
non-duality and non-trinity.*

September 29

'O monks, let each of you see into his own mind. Do not memorize what I tell you. However eloquently I may talk about all kinds of things as innumerable as the sands of the Ganges, the mind shows no increase; even when no talk is possible, the mind shows no decrease. You may talk ever so much about it, and it is still your own mind; you may not at all talk about it, and it is just the same as your own mind. You may divide your body into so many forms, and emitting rays of supernatural light perform the eighteen miracles, and yet what you have gained is after all no more than your own dead ashes.'

September 30

The more talking and thinking,
the farther from the truth.
Cutting off all speech, all thought,
there is nowhere that you cannot go.

October

October 1

If a man with overall sameness
conforms his mind to the
Buddha doctrines
and enters the non-dual Buddha's gate
that man is difficult for thought
to judge.

October 2

An unenlightened and bewildered life rises out of a mind that is bewildered by its own creation of a world of delusion outside of the mind. When bewildered minds become clear and cease to create impure surroundings, they attain enlightenment.

October 3

People grasp after things for their own imagined convenience and comfort; they grasp after wealth and treasure and honours; they cling desperately to life; they make arbitrary distinctions between good and bad, right and wrong, and then vehemently affirm and deny them.

October 4

*To set up what you like against
what you dislike —
that is disease of the mind:
when the deep meaning of the Way
is not understood,
peace of mind is disturbed
to no purpose.*

October 5

*When oneness is not
thoroughly understood,
in two ways loss is sustained:
the denying of reality is
the asserting of it,
and the asserting of emptiness
is the denying of it.*

October 6

All forms of dualism
are contrived by the
ignorant themselves.
They are like unto visions
and flowers in the air:
why should we trouble to
take hold of them?
Gain and loss, right and wrong –
away with them once and for all!

October 7

In my house there is a cave,
and in the cave there is nothing at all —
pure and wonderfully empty,
resplendent with light like the sun,
a meal of greens will do for
this old body,
a ragged coat will cover this
phantom form.
Let a thousand saints appear
before me —
I have the Buddha of
Heavenly Truth!

October 8

Evil is born in the mind and
in the mind destroyed.

October 9

*If you perceive both self
and Buddhahood
as remaining in the sign of sameness,
then you will reside in no-residing
and be far beyond all things that exist.*

October 10

How sad that people ignore the near
and search for truth afar.

October 11

Time flies quicker than an arrow and life passes with greater transience than the dew. However skilful you may be, how can you ever recall a single day of the past?

All objects, all worlds, all facts in the world, this body, this treasure, this dwelling, are all appearances that have arisen because of the activities of delusions that are inherent within their own mental appearances.

October 13

Obey the nature of things, and
you are in concord with
the Way, calm and easy,
free from annoyance;
but when your thoughts are tied,
you turn away from the truth,
they grow heavier and duller
and not at all sound.

October 14

All things good or bad, beautiful or
ugly – should be treated as void.
Even in time of disputes and quarrels
we should treat our intimates and our
enemies alike and never think
of retaliation.

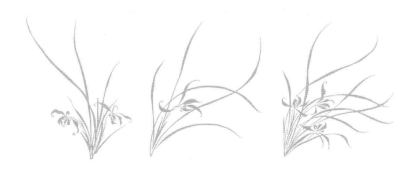

October 15

The phenomena of light and dark alternate
with each other, but the nature of the void
remains unchanged. So it is with the Mind of
the Buddha and of sentient beings. If you
look upon the Buddha as presenting a pure,
bright or enlightened appearance, or upon
sentient beings as presenting a foul, dark or
mortal-seeming appearance, these
attachments to form will keep you from
supreme knowledge, even after the passing
of as many aeons as there are sands in
the Ganges.

October 16

Yajnadatta, a citizen of Sravasti, one morning looked into the mirror and found a face with charming features. He thought his own head had disappeared and thereby went crazy. This story is used to illustrate the stupidity of clinging to relative knowledge which arises from the opposition of subject and object. As we cling to it as having absolute value, a world of topsy-turviness extends before us. The original bright and charming face is ours only when we realize the fact by reflecting within ourselves, instead of running after unrealities.

October 17

The master once said, 'Our school lets you go any way you like. It kills and it brings to life – either way.'

A monk then asked, 'How does it kill?'

The master replied, 'Winter goes and Spring comes.'

'How,' asked the monk, 'is it when Winter goes and Spring comes?'

The master said, 'Shouldering your staff, you wander this way and that, East or West, South or North, knocking on the wild stumps as you please.'

October 18

Over the river the shining moon;
in the pine trees, sighing wind;
all night long so tranquil – why?
And for whom?

October 19

If one understands all the elements –
that nothing exists in the perceiver,
that perceived elements are
nothing, too –
then one can illuminate the world.

October 20

Here is a tree older than the forest itself;
the years of its life defy reckoning.
Its roots have seen the upheavals
of hill and valley;
its leaves have known the changes
of wind and frost.
The world laughs at its shoddy exterior
and cares nothing for the fine grain
of the wood inside.
Stripped free of flesh and hide,
all that remains is the core of truth.

October 21

The ego-self and the idea of possession have no true existence. There is only the age-old habit of erroneous thinking that leads people to perceive and to discriminate various aspects of the world where in reality there are none.

October 22

Snow that we two
saw together –
this year is it fallen anew?

October 23

You must concentrate on Zen practice without wasting time, thinking that there is only this day and this hour. After that it becomes truly easy. You must forget about the good or the bad of your nature, the strength and the weakness of your power.

October 24

When Toukusan gained an insight into the truth of Zen, he immediately took out all his commentaries on the Diamond Sutra and set fire to them. They were once so valuable and indispensable that he carried them with him wherever he went,.

He exclaimed: 'However deep one's knowledge of philosophy, it is like a piece of hair flying in space; however important one's experience in worldly things, it is like a drop of water thrown into an unfathomable abyss.'

*He neither seeks the true nor severs
himself from the defiled,
he clearly perceives that dualities are
empty and have no reality,
that to have no reality means not
to be one-sided, neither empty
nor not-empty,
for this is the genuine form of
Tathagatahood.*

October 26

Ummon Bunen wanted his followers to be very clear and definite in what they were doing, and to illustrate this he said, 'When you sit, sit; when you walk, walk. Above all, don't wobble.'

October 27

Whence is my life?
Whither does it go?
I sit alone in my hut
and meditate quietly;
with all my thinking I know nowhere,
nor do I come to any whither:
such is my present,
eternally changing – all in emptiness!
In this emptiness the ego
rests for a while,
with it yeas and nays;
I know not where to set them up,
I follow my karma *as it moves, in*
perfect contentment.

October 28

Returning to the root,
we get the essence;
following after appearances,
we lose the spirit.
If for only a moment, we see within,
we have surpassed the
emptiness of things.
Changes that go on in this emptiness
all arise because of our ignorance.

October 29

For people life is a succession of
graspings and attachments and then,
because of it, they assume the illusion
of pain and suffering.

October 30

'I truly attained nothing from complete, unexcelled enlightenment.'

It was for fear that people would not believe this that the Buddha drew upon what is seen with five sorts of vision and spoken with five kinds of speech. So this quotation is by no means empty at all, but expresses the highest truth.

October 31

All you have to do is realize that birth
and death, as such, should not be
avoided and then they will cease to
exist, for if you can understand that
birth and death are *nirvana* itself
there is not only no necessity to avoid
them but also nothing to search for
that is called *nirvana*.

November

November 1

Not a single thought arising,
empty yet perceptive,
still, yet illuminating,
complete like the Great Emptiness
containing all that is wonderful.

November 2

During the period before the world was manifested there were no names. The moment the Buddha arrives in the world there are names and so we clutch hold of forms. In the great *Tao* there is absolutely nothing secular or sacred. If there are names, everything is classified in limits and bounds.

November 3

Keep your mind alive and free without abiding in anything or anywhere.

November 4

Form and sensation are
without number
so are conception, thought and
consciousness.
He who understands that is so,
that man is the great solitary saint.

November 5

The human mind discriminates itself from the things that appear to be outside itself without first realizing that it has first created these very things within its own mind. This has been going on from beginningless time and the delusion has become firmly fixed within the mind and even adheres things to themselves.

Those who act in evil, selfish ways suffer not only the natural consequences of the acts, but are followed by the thought: 'I have done wrong,' and the memory of the act is stored in *karma* to work out its inevitable retribution in following lives.

November 7

When you strive to gain quiescence
by stopping motion,
the quiescence thus gained
is ever in motion;
as long as you tarry in dualism,
how can you realize oneness?

November 8

Sleet falling;
fathomless, infinite
loneliness.

357

November 9

People are afraid to forget their
ordinary, dualistic minds, fearing to fall
through Emptiness with nothing to
stay their fall. They do not know that
Emptiness is not really empty, but the
realm of the real way.

Zen opens a man's eyes to the greatest
mystery as it is daily and hourly
performed; it enlarges the heart to
embrace the eternity of time
and the infinity of space
in its every palpitation;
it makes us live in the world as if
walking in the garden of Eden.

November 11

*Among a thousand clouds
and ten thousand streams,
here lives an idle man,
in the daytime wandering
over green mountains,
at night coming home
to sleep by the cliff.
Swiftly the springs and autumns pass,
but my mind is at peace,
free from dust or delusion.
How pleasant to know
I need nothing to lean on,
to be still as the waters
of the autumn river.*

November 12

*If a person thinks true enlightenment
is release from the influxes,
and detachment from things
of the world
he does not possess the true of truth.*

November 13

When an artist draws a picture the details are filled in from his own mind and a single picture is capable of an infinity of detail; so the human mind fills in the surroundings of its life.

November 14

In Buddhism the un-born is the un-
dying. Life is a position of time. Death
is a position of time. They are like
winter and spring. We do not consider
that winter becomes spring, or that
spring becomes summer.

November 15

In the one he understands the countless.
In the countless he understands the one.
Evolving lives are not reality.
For the man who is wise there is
no fear.

November 16

Taoshin came and bowed to Sengtsan, and
said, 'I will ask you for your merciful
teaching. Please show me how to be released.'
Sengtsan answered, 'Who has bound you?'
'No one,' he replied.
Sengtsan said, 'Why then do you ask
to be released?'
Taoshin immediately came to a
profound realization.

November 17

We sleep with both legs outstretched,
free of the true, free of the false.

November 18

If people can change their viewpoints,
can break up these age-old habits of
thinking, can rid their minds of desires
and infatuations and egoism, then the
wisdom of true enlightenment
is possible.

November 19

No one can live your life except you.
No one can live my life except me.
You are responsible. I am responsible.
But what is our life? What is our death?

November 20

On a journey, ill –
and my dreams, on withered fields
are wandering still.

Should you live for a hundred years
just wasting your time, every day
will be filled with sorrow;
should you drift as the slave
of your senses for a hundred years
and yet live truly for only so much
as a single day you will in that one
day not only live a hundred years
of life but also a hundred years
of your future life.

November 22

*Whoever perceives that all the Buddhas
appear in the world in the same instant
and yet nothing really arises
that person has a great reputation.*

November 23

There is only one mind and not a particle of anything else on which to lay hold, for this mind is the Buddha. If you students of the Way do not awake to this mind substance, you will overlay mind with conceptual thought, you will seek the Buddha outside yourself, and you will remain attached to forms.

*Where mind and each believing
mind are not divided,
and undivided are each believing mind
and mind,
this is where words fail;
for it is not of the past, present
and future.*

Ananda wants to know how to get into a palatial mansion, which he is told is to be his own. The Buddha says there are two methods to effect the entrance, and these must be practised conjointly. The one is Samatha *or 'tranquillization', the other* Vipasyana *or 'contemplation'.*

November 26

The long night;
the sound of water
says what I think.

November 27

Like the clear stillness of autumn water
– pure and without activity; in its
tranquil depths are no obstructions.
Such a one is called a man of *Tao*, also
a man who has nothing further to do.

November 28

Ken-o and his disciple, Menzan, were eating a melon together. Suddenly the master asked, 'Tell me, where does all the sweetness come from?'

'Why,' Menzan quickly swallowed and answered, 'it's a product of cause and effect.'

'Bah! That's cold logic!'

'Well,' Menzan said, 'from where then?'

'From the very "where" itself, that's where.'

November 29

It is considered that the old Chinese Zen masters . . . saw everything in nature as interrelated with everything else and so did not regard some as good and others as bad, or some as superior or higher and others as inferior and lower. This is quite in agreement with modern science also, by which we can say that everything is what it is and where it is because of everything else – and itself.

November 30

*To set up what you like against
what you dislike –
this is the disease of the mind;
when the deep meaning of the
Way is not understood
peace of mind is disturbed to
no purpose.*

December

December 1

The Way is perfect like unto vast space,
with nothing wanting,
nothing superfluous,
it is indeed due to making choice
that its Suchness is lost sight of.

December 2

*The ignorant cherish the idea
of rest and unrest,
the unenlightened have likes
and dislikes.*

December 3

No one lives at the Barrier of Fuha;
the wooden penthouse is fallen away;
all that remains
is the autumn wind.

December 4

All things being empty, so is the mind. As the mind is empty, all is. My mind is not divisible: all is contained in my every thought which appears as enlightenment to the wise, illusion to the stupid. Yet enlightenment and illusion are one. Do away with both, but don't remain 'in between' either. In this way you will be emptiness itself which, stainless and devoid of the interrelationships of things, transcends realization. In this way the true Zen priest commonly conducts himself.

December 5

When the ancient Zen master was asked about the meaning of Buddhism he replied, 'If there is any meaning in it, I myself am not liberated.'

December 6

One day, Jizo received one of Hofuku's disciples and asked him, 'How does your teacher instruct you?'
'My teacher instructs me to shut my eyes and see no evil thing; to cover my ears and hear no evil sound; to stop my mind-activities and form no wrong ideas,' the monk replied.
'I do not ask you to shut your eyes,' Jizo said, 'but you do not see a thing. I do not ask you to cover your ears, but you do not hear a sound. I do not ask you to cease your mind-activities, but you do not form any idea at all.'

December 7

*Scoop up the water and the moon
is in your hands;
hold the flowers and your clothes
are scented with them.*

December 8

*To save life it must be destroyed
when utterly destroyed, one dwells for
the first time in peace.*

December 9

In the true essence there is neither samskrita *(created) nor* asamkrita *(uncreated); they are like* maya *or flowers born of hallucination. When you attempt to manifest what is true by means of what is erroneous, you make both untrue. When you endeavour to explain object by subject and subject by object, you create a world of endless opposites; nothing real is grasped. To experience perfect interfusion, let all the opposites be dissolved. When there is clinging of any sort, and an ego-mind is asserted, the essence dissipates and the mysterious lotus fades.*

December 10

The skylark:
its voice alone fell
leaving nothing behind.

December 11

In the deep mystery of this
'things as they are',
we are released from our
relations to them.
When all things are seen
'with equal mind',
they return to their nature.

December 12

When there is no duality,
all things are one,
there is nothing that is not included.
The Enlightened of all times and places
have all entered into this Truth.

December 13

When you are silent, it speaks;
when you speak, it is silent.
The great gate is open to bestow alms,
and no crowd is blocking the Way.

December 14

Heaven and Earth and I are of the same root, the ten-thousand things and I are of one substance.

December 15

The doctrine of fearlessness is taught as loudly as a lion roars: what a pity that confused minds, inflexibly hardened like leather, understand only that grave offences are obstructions to enlightenment, and are unable to see into the secrets of the Tathagata's teaching.

December 16

Do not build up your views on your senses and thoughts, do not carry on your understanding based on your senses and thoughts; but at the same time do not seek the mind away from your senses and thoughts, do not grasp the *Dharma* by rejecting your senses and thoughts. When you are neither attached to nor detached from them, when you are neither abiding with nor clinging to them, then you enjoy your perfect unobstructed freedom, then you have your seat of enlightenment.

December 17

*The two exist because of the one,
but hold not even to this one;
when the mind is not disturbed,
ten thousand things offer no offence.*

December 18

Both delusion and enlightenment originate in the mind, and every fact arises from the activities of the mind just as different things arise from the sleeve of the magician.

December 19

Tao-wu asked: 'What is the
ultimate teaching of Buddhism?'
'You won't understand it
until you have it.'
'Is there anything over and above it
whereby one may have a new turn?'
'Boundlessly expands the sky and
nothing obstructs the white clouds
from freely flying about.'

December 20

Without enlightenment there would be no difference between a Buddha and other living beings; while a gleam of enlightenment is enough to make any living being the equal of a Buddha. Since all *dharmas* are immanent in our mind there is no reason why we should not realize intuitively the real nature of suchness.

December 21

*The wind brings
fallen leaves enough
to make a fire.*

My mind is like the autumn moon
shining clean and clear
in the green pool.
No, that's not a good comparison.
Tell me, how shall I explain?

December 23

There is no place to seek the mind;
it is like the footprints of the birds
in the sky.

December 24

Zen enlightenment is as if you have been far away from home for many years, when you suddenly see your father in town. You know him right away without a doubt. There is no need to ask whether he is your father or not.

December 25

When in Zen there is the advice to give up all concepts, it must of course include the concept of no concept.

December 26

Awakening is where there is no birth, no extinction; it is seeing into the state of Suchness, absolutely transcending all the categories of constructed mind.

December 27

Always Zen is to be found, if at all,
in immediate experience, the firefly
rather than the star.

December 28

Suppose a warrior, forgetting that he was already wearing his pearl on his forehead, were to seek for it elsewhere, he could travel the whole world without finding it. But if someone who knew what was wrong were to point to him, the warrior would immediately realize that the pearl had been there all the time.

December 29

*The old pine tree speaks
divine wisdom;
the secret bird manifests
eternal truth.*

December 30

When you really hear the sound of rain
you can hear and see and feel
everything in the same way –
as needing no translation, as being
just what it is, though it may be
impossible to say what.

December 31

*The Way is perfect
like unto vast space,
with nothing wanting,
nothing superfluous,
it is indeed due to making a choice
that its suchness is lost sight of.*

413

SOURCES

Blofield, John *The Zen Teaching of Huang Po*, Buddhist Society, 1958

Blyth, R.H. *The Young East*, R. H. Blyth, Tokyo, 1954

– *Zen and Zen Classics*, Hokuseido Press, Tokyo, 1960

– Zen in English Literature and Oriental Culture, Hokusaido Press, 1942

Burt, E.A. (ed.) *The Teachings of the Compassionate Buddha* (trans. Dr. Liebenthal), American Library of World Literature, 1955

Chen-tao Ke *Song of the Realisation of the Way* (trans. Suzuki, Senzaki and McCandless), 1950

Chiang-te Ch'uan-teng Lu *Record of the Transmission of the Lamp*

Chinese Buddhist Verse (trans. Richard Robinson), John Murray, 1954

Conze, E. & Casssirer, B. (eds) *Buddhist Texts Through the Ages*, Oxford, 1954

Gendo Nakai Kanao Bunendo, *Shinran and his Religion of Pure Faith*, Kyoto, 1946

Huang Po *The Doctrine of Universal Mind* (trans. Chu Cha'an) Buddhist Society, London, 1937

– *Manual of Zen Buddhism* (trans. D. T. Suzuki), Eastern Buddhist Society, 1935

The Zen Teachings of Huang Po (trans. John Blofield), Rider, 1958

Huxley, Aldous *Lankavatra Sutra in The Perennial Philosophy*, Chatto and Windus, 1955

Anthology of Japanese Literature, Allen and Unwin, 1956

Masanuga, R. *A Primer in Soto Zen*, Routledge and Kegan Paul, 1972

Ogata, Sohaku *Zen for the West*, Rider, 1959

Seng-tsan *Essays in Zen Buddhism* (trans D.T. Suzuki), Luzac, 1927

Senzake, Nyogen *Buddhism and Zen*, North Point Press, 1987

– (ed.), *Zen Flesh, Zen Bones: A Collection of Zen and pre-Zen Writings*, Shambhala Publications, 1957

– and Ruth Strout, *Buddhism and Zen*, McCandless Philosophical Library, New York,1953

Stryck, Lucien *Zen: Poems, Prayers, Sermons, Anecdotes, Interviews*, Doubleday, 1963

Suzuki, D.T. *Zen Doctrines of No Mind*, Rider ,1969

– *Essays in Zen Buddhism*, Luzac, 1933

– *Manual of Zen Buddhism*, Grove Press ,1960

– *Studies in the Lankavatara Sutra*, Routledge and Kegan Paul, 1972

– *Studies in Zen*, Dell, 1955

– *Zen and Japanese Culture*, Princeton University Press, 1959

Thoreau, Henry David *Walden,* Konemann, 1995

The Wang Ling Record

Watts, Alan W. *The Way of Zen*, Pantheon Books, New York, 1957

Sutra of Wei Leung (trans. Wong Mou-lam), Luzac and Co., 1944

Wood, E. *Zen Dictionary*, Penguin, 1957

Wu-men Kuan *The Barrier Without Gate* (trans. Nyogen Senezaki and Paul Reps)

Zen Poems of China and Japan: the Crane's Bill, compiled and translated by Lucien Stryk and Takashi Ikemoto, Grove Press, 1973

The Penguin Book of Zen Poetry (trans. Lucien Stryk and Takashi Ikemoto), Penguin

DISCLAIMER